What do we mean by human rights?

Freedom
of Speech

Philip Steele

W
FRANKLIN WATTS
LONDON • NEW YORK • SYDNEY

This edition 2000

First published in 1997
by Franklin Watts
96 Leonard Street, London
EC2A 4RH

Franklin Watts Australia
14 Mars Road
Lane Cove
NSW 2066

© Franklin Watts 1997

Series editor: Rachel Cooke
Art Director: Robert Walster
Designer: Simon Borrough
Picture research: Sarah Moule
Consultants: Cristina Sganga and
Dan Jones of Amnesty International

A CIP catalogue record for this book
is available from the British Library.

ISBN 0 7496 2378 0 (hbk)
ISBN 0 7496 3824 9 (pbk)

Dewey Classification 323.44
Printed in Italy

Acknowledgments:
Case studies: Australia, *Melbourne
Age/Index on Censorship 25.2*, 1996;
South Africa, *Children Under
Apartheid*, London,1980; Denmark,
Berlingske Tidende/Reuter/*Index on
Censorship 25.3*, 1996; USA, Philippa
Nugent/statistics from Office of
Intellectual Freedom, American Library
Association/*Index on Censorship 25.2*,
1996; Canada, *International Herald
Tribune/Index on Censorship 25.2*,
1996; Egypt, *Index on Censorship
25.2*, 1996; UK, *Censorship*, Wolmar
(Wayland, 1990); Bangladesh, *Info 96*,
Hutchinson Gallup; Croatia, World
Service BBC/*Index on Censorshp 25.2*,
1996; Philippines, Reporters Sans
Frontières/*Index on Censorship 25.2*,
1996; Guatemala, Amnesty
International/*Index on Censorship
25.3*, 1996, Myanmar, *Info 96*,
Hutchinson Gallup; Ivory Coast,
Reporters Sans Frontières/*Index on
Censorship 25.2*, 1996

Picture credits:

The authors would like to thank
the following for their permission
to reproduce the photographs in
this book:

Cover image: Hutchison Library
Insides: AKG London pp. 7t (Prado
Museum, Madrid), 35t
Mary Evans Picture Library pp. 10b,
12t, 35b
Ronald Grant Archive pp. 14
(Courtesy Castle Rock/Turner), 25b
(Courtesy Orion)
Robert Harding Picture Library pp. 6l
(Delimage), 19b, 20
Hulton Getty Collection p. 12b
Hutchison Library pp. 5, 11
Image Bank p. 22b
Magnum Photos pp. 6r (Richard
Kalvar), 7b (Paul Lowe), 15r (Rene
Burri), 16/17 (Gideon Mendel), 22t
(Eli Reed), 24 (Paul Fusco), 26l (F.
Scianna), 32 (Peter Marlow), 34
(James Nachtwey), 38t (Stuart
Franklin), 38b (Leonard Freed), 39 (F.
Mayer), 40b (Stuart Franklin), 41
(Steve McCurry), 42b (Raghu Rai)
Mansell Collection p. 9
Panos Pictures pp. 10t (Penny
Tweedie), 16t (Barbara Klass), 42t
(Chris Stowers)
Popperfoto pp. 8, 28
Rex Features pp. 15l , 16b, 17 (Greg
Williams), 18 (Sipa Press), 19t
(Martin Beddall), 20/21 (Sipa Press),
21 (Brendan Beirne), 23l (Sipa Press),
23r (Adrian Brooks), 25t, 27b, 29l
(Peter Brooker), 29r (Sipa Press), 30t
(Gamma), 30b, 31 (Martin Beddall),
33 (Sipa Press), 37, 43
Topham pp. 8/9 (Associated
Press/Greg English), 13t (Press
Association), 13b, 26r (Associated
Press), 27t (Press Association), 36t
(Associated Press), 36b
Janine Wiedel, p. 40t

CONTENTS

From the moment we are born we communicate. When we are babies we gurgle or cry to tell our parents when we are happy or hungry. Soon we learn to speak and to understand words. And as we grow, we learn to put together whole sentences and to read and write.

The need to communicate

Communication is how we keep in touch with other human beings. If people are trapped in a cave or stranded on a lonely desert island, they soon lose their health and happiness and even their sense of who they are. Every day, people all over the world communicate – by arguing, gossiping, chatting, singing songs, teaching and learning, talking on the telephone, writing letters or sending faxes or e-mail.

People can also communicate without words. They may smile or frown, raise their eyebrows to show surprise, hug each other in friendship or thump the table in anger. Painting pictures, dancing and making music are also ways of communicating without words. Throughout history people have also invented many different ways of exchanging messages – by signalling with flags, whistles or drums, flashing mirrors or clouds of smoke. Even prisoners, locked alone in a cell, have learned to communicate with each other by knocking on the walls of their cell.

'every day people all over the world communicate'

A mother communicates with her baby by talking, singing, smiling, laughing and touching. Whenever people talk to each other they may make their message clearer by shrugging their shoulders, by making gestures with their hands or pulling faces. We all need to communicate with each other to survive.

Artists can put across powerful visual messages. In *The 3rd May 1808*, the Spanish artist Francisco Goya (1746-1828) expresses his horror and grief at the death of his fellow countrymen, shot by French soldiers for rebelling against French rule of their country.

Communication is any exchange of information, ideas, beliefs or feelings.

'communication is any exchange of information'

It is this ability to exchange very complex messages and signals that sets human beings apart from other living creatures on the planet. Some of the information we exchange may be day-to-day chat with friends, of little interest to anyone else. But other information may be important to all kinds of people. Every one of us needs to discuss news, political ideas, religious beliefs and scientific discoveries if we are to take part in the society in which we live and make it work.

Japanese travellers stop for a quick telephone call before catching their trains. Modern communications have completely changed the way we keep in touch with each other – and the way we live.

Making ourselves heard

If we have ideas we want to put across to a large number of people, we have to call a public meeting, write a book or a newspaper article, talk on radio or television or use the internet. All the different methods we can use to communicate are called the media. Any one of these methods is called a medium of communication.

From 1976 to 1983 Argentina was ruled by its armed forces. Many people who objected and spoke up for democracy 'disappeared', that is, they were arrested and secretly murdered. In 1995, these women were demanding to know the names of those who had died.

(Below) Women cast their vote in Iran in the presidential election of 1989, so expressing their views on who should run their country.

A say in government

Publishing, broadcasting and performance are not the only ways of putting across ideas. A vote in a general election is also a way of communicating. It is a way of expressing choice, of saying 'These are the people I would like to govern the country'. A society or country which is ruled by a government chosen by the people who belong to it is called a democracy.

The word 'democracy' comes from ancient Greek words meaning 'rule by the people'. However, throughout history, people have been unable to agree exactly what 'rule by the people' should mean or how it should be put into practice. When Greek rulers introduced democracy to Athens in 508 BC, they only gave the vote to men. Women, slaves and foreigners who lived permanently in the city did not get the vote, even though these three groups formed the majority of the population.

A truly democratic government should be one created by and for free expression. There should be two-way communication between all the citizens and the government. In practice that communication frequently breaks down. In extreme cases, when this communication breaks down it can lead to a dictatorship, in which one person rules the country and the people have no say at all in how they are governed.

'rule by the people'

Date: 399 BC
Place: Athens, Greece
Issue: Teaching new ideas

In 399 BC a philosopher from Athens drank a cup of poison and died. He was called Socrates and he had been sentenced to death by the authorities. His only crime had been to get his students to ask difficult questions about the world and how it worked. He was accused of being a troublemaker, of spreading dangerous new ideas, and of teaching young people not to respect the traditional Greek gods.

This 18th-century painting shows Socrates about to take poison. Although his ideas were considered corrupting by the ancient Greek authorities, Socrates has long since been recognized as a ground-breaking philosopher and thinker.

Changing the way we think

Communication without interference from anyone else is called freedom of speech. This term is often used to include all kinds of communication and expression, not just the spoken word. Free speech is necessary to bring about change in all kinds of ways. Scientists need to be able to publish their discoveries and details of their inventions. Teachers and philosophers should be able to pass on their ideas to new generations of students.

9

European settlers in Australia saw the Aboriginal people as savages, as reflected in images like this one (right), and treated them badly. Now some Aboriginal people are using their strong artistic tradition to express their anger about their treatment.

Going public

Many artists try to change the way in which people see the world, offering their private visions to the public. Throughout history, books, plays, and even operas, have been written to make fun of powerful people or criticize the way people behave. New ideas may be expressed which are unpopular or shocking. They may upset governments or religious leaders. This may lead to the authors or artists being persecuted and their works destroyed. But many feel they have a moral responsibility to speak up.

'new ideas may be shocking'

A human right?

Freedom of speech or expression is so important that most people agree that it is a human right. A right is a claim for a basic need to be recognized and dealt with fairly by other people. It might be said that all humans have a right to freedom, justice, education and health, and to choose the way they are governed. Since most of these rights depend on people being able to communicate freely, freedom of speech has to be one of the most important rights of all.

Date: 1996
Place: Melbourne, Australia
Issue: Art that shocks

Melbourne city council asked an Aboriginal artist called Ray Thomas to produce works in honour of the history of his people, but in January 1996 withdrew five of them for being too shocking. One, intended for the Supreme Court building, showed an Aboriginal's head pierced by the Sword of Justice. The artist felt this reflected the long history of injustice and discrimination suffered by the Aboriginal people at the hands of the European settlers. The Chief Justice of the State of Victoria complained that it was unsuitable as it did not show respect for the rule of law.

During the World War II (1939-45) many human rights were brutally ignored. That was one reason why in 1948 the United Nations decided to draw up a list of the basic rights shared by human beings around the world. It included the right to freedom of expression. The same right was included in the UN Convention on the Rights of the Child, which was internationally adopted in 1989. The key articles from both declarations are given in full in the panel.

This book explores what it means to have the right to free speech and how that right is upheld and abused around the world today.

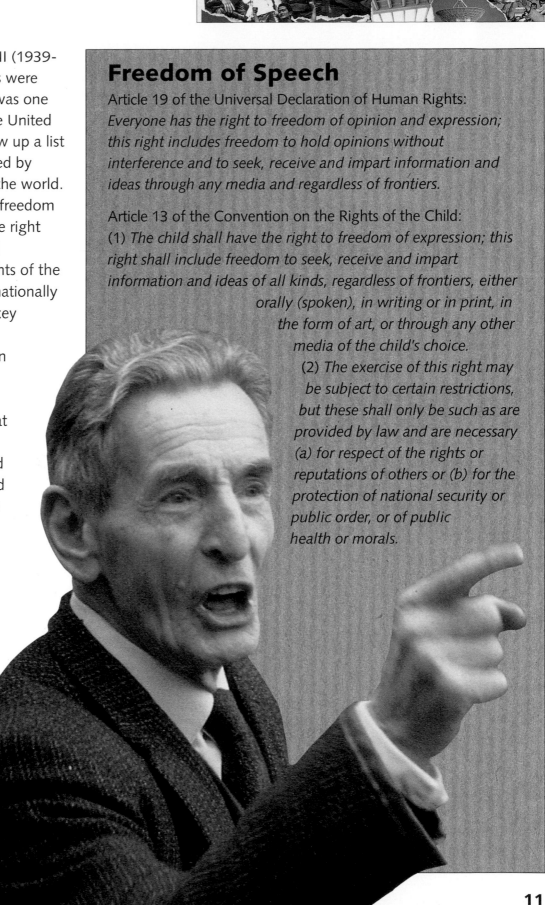

Speakers' Corner in London is famous for free speaking. Anyone can stand up there and speak to the public on any subject they choose.

Freedom of Speech

Article 19 of the Universal Declaration of Human Rights:
Everyone has the right to freedom of opinion and expression; this right includes freedom to hold opinions without interference and to seek, receive and impart information and ideas through any media and regardless of frontiers.

Article 13 of the Convention on the Rights of the Child:
(1) *The child shall have the right to freedom of expression; this right shall include freedom to seek, receive and impart information and ideas of all kinds, regardless of frontiers, either orally (spoken), in writing or in print, in the form of art, or through any other media of the child's choice.*
(2) The exercise of this right may be subject to certain restrictions, but these shall only be such as are provided by law and are necessary (a) for respect of the rights or reputations of others or (b) for the protection of national security or public order, or of public health or morals.

Date:
14 July 1870
Place:
Bad Ems, Germany
Issue:
Twisting the message

In 1870 Germany was not one country but separated into many different states. The most powerful of these, Prussia, wanted to unite Germany and felt war with France would help achieve this goal. The argument between the two countries came to a head when it was suggested that a cousin of Wilhelm I, the Prussian king, should become king of Spain. The French objected and the Prussians agreed not to go ahead with the plan. The French then made further demands and sent their ambassador to see Wilhelm I, who was on holiday at the town of Bad Ems.

A magazine cartoon of Otto von Bismarck in 1870. A ruthless politician, Bismarck was nicknamed the Iron Chancellor.

Wilhelm I was polite to the French ambassador. Afterwards he sent a telegram describing the meeting to the head of his government, Otto von Bismarck. Bismarck made public the contents of the telegram, but cunningly left out certain sections. As a result he made it sound as if the king and the ambassador had quarrelled and insulted each other.

The French were furious. Without making proper preparations, they declared war on Prussia on 19 July – falling into Bismarck's trap. By 1 September the French had been disastrously defeated. German unification followed soon after.

Prussian troops line up their gun carriages on the streets of Paris. Bismarck's cunning reworking of the Bad Ems telegram paid off: not only did it bring victory over the French but also, impressed by Prussian power, the other German states agreed to unite under Prussian control, so forming the modern state of Germany.

A journalist works on screen, writing, deleting or moving text. All communication is edited or controlled to some extent.

Making the point

To a large extent the way we communicate and express ourselves is decided by the medium we are using. If we are phoning in to a radio programme, putting on a play, or writing an article in a scientific journal, we use the type of language suitable for that particular medium and the people who will hear, see or read it. If we do not, we may not get our message across.

The message communicated by an artist who uses thick oil paint in bold colours will be very different from that made by one using, say, delicate water colour paints or laser beams in a darkened room.

'We are anxious to put our message across in the best possible way'

The same but different

Bismarck's actions show just how powerful words can be. Words can be moved and changed or left out to give different shades of meaning. We do it ourselves every day. As we talk, we change our tone or our expression according to whom we are talking or the point we are making. We may leave out certain parts of a story that reflect badly upon ourselves or other people. We are anxious to put our message across in the best possible way. When we write a letter or a report we do the same: deciding what to put in and what to leave out. Sometimes we may go further and tell a half-truth or even a lie. Similar processes take place within the media. As an author types the words of a book, he or she will change them, delete them or move them to another chapter. Later, editors read through these words and make changes that they think are necessary. There are many reasons for editing a text, or a radio or television programme: to make it more accurate, easier to read, or to alter its message or bias. In Bismarck's case, he edited a telegram to provoke an argument.

A broadcaster takes calls from the public live on air. This communication takes in many different people: the caller, the broadcaster, the radio audience and the programme's producer, who may cut off any caller who becomes abusive.

Date: 1818
Place: England
Issue: Changing attitudes and tastes

In 1818 a new edition of the works of William Shakespeare was published. Its editor was an Englishman called Thomas Bowdler.

Bowdler loved the works of Shakespeare but was shocked by the way the poet included sex, violence and swearing. He thought the play *Othello* so shocking that he recommended that it be locked away in a cupboard rather than left in the sitting room where women or children might see it. He decided to edit Shakespeare's plays so they could be 'read aloud by all the family'. He cut out large sections of the original texts, making characters exclaim 'Heavens!' instead of 'God!'.

The new *Family Shakespeare* sold well in both Britain and the United States. Today, most people consider his edition old-fashioned and Shakespeare's work is studied in the language he wrote it. But we still use the word 'bowdlerize' to describe the unnecessary cleaning up, or expurgation, of a book.

A scene from a film of William Shakespeare's Othello. To Thomas Bowdler, this play was too shocking to be read by children. Today it is widely studied in schools.

A wider audience

Although communication is about linking us, as individuals, with other people, we are all part of a wider society, and that also affects the way we communicate. Every society has controls and rules: they may be written rules in the form of laws, or unwritten rules that reflect the general attitudes of the time. These, too, influence what we say and how we say it. Bowdler's edition of Shakespeare reflected the moral attitudes of 19th-century Britain. Today attitudes to sex and strong language are rather more relaxed and people generally consider Bowdler's actions unnecessary. But there are still many people who find some of Shakespeare's plays 'unsuitable' for children. Within every society, people have different opinions about what its rules, written and unwritten, should be.

Money talks

Having money makes it much easier to get your message across. People with money have power and access to the media, that is, they can make their ideas public if they want to. What is more, the media are generally more interested in the views of rich and famous individuals than in those of people on the street.

The businessman Rupert Murdoch (above) heads a worldwide media empire made up of newspapers, publishing and satellite TV companies. This gives him considerable power not only to express his point of view but also to influence other people's.

'to enable them to receive and impart information'

The head of a big company will probably be able to put across his or her viewpoint or message on television and a rich newspaper owner may be able to use his or her newspapers to influence what people read. For example, the political beliefs and sympathies of the owner may be reflected in the way news stories are reported. Some people worry about the power newspaper owners have over public opinion.

The coming of radio and TV has made it easier for people all over the world to receive information, but it is not always so easy for them to send or 'impart' information. How can ordinary people make their voices heard?

People with little money or influence find it very hard to make their opinions heard. It is much more difficult for them to gain access to the media to express their views. Giving people this access to the media – to enable them to receive and impart information – is an important part of giving them freedom of expression.

Education and knowledge

Education is important if people are to benefit fully from the media. Many people in the world are illiterate. In the African

This boy in Bangladesh is learing to write. The right to free communication depends on the right to education.

countries of Sierra Leone and Guinea and in the Asian state of Bhutan, over three-quarters of the adult population have not been taught to read or write. In the United States one in every hundred people is illiterate. Such people are unable to make full use of modern communications media, and also face great problems in finding jobs, filling in forms and all the many other things literate people take for granted.

Knowledge and experience also help us evaluate for ourselves what we read, see or hear. If we are reading about events in another part of the world about which we know very little, how can we judge whether the report is accurate or not? Or when two politicians draw different conclusions from the same event, how can we decide who is right? We have to rely on our education, experience and judgement. We soon learn not to believe everything we read, hear or see in the media.

Reading a newspaper helps us form our opinions, even if we don't agree with its viewpoint.

Date:
16 June 1976
Place:
Soweto, South Africa
Issue:
Which language in the classroom?

In 1976 South Africa was still ruled only by white people, although the majority of the people living there were black or of mixed-race. The government said that in future black and mixed-race

Children led many of the protests that finally brought change to South Africa.

schoolchildren would have to be taught many of their lessons in the Afrikaans language. However the children still wanted to be taught in English, which they could understand more easily.

On 16 June a young boy called Hector Peterson joined his friends in a big demonstration on the streets of Soweto. The South African police tear-gassed the crowds and shot many of the children, wounding and killing them. Hector was the first to die.

The language we speak

The language we use is another factor that affects communication. Some languages are understood by more people than others, while other languages may be ignored by the media or by governments. About 5,300 languages are spoken around the world, but only 80 of them are officially approved by governments or law courts. In some countries, some languages are banned from everyday use, from schools or the media. Hector Peterson was victim of one such ban.

Other ways to communicate

Many people find it hard to communicate because they are deaf or dumb or blind. They have had to invent other ways of communicating. People who cannot speak or hear may sign with their hands. Blind people may use Braille. People who communicate in this way may find it hard to put their views across to the public, and may find themselves ignored by the media. In recent years many disabled people have worked hard to ensure that their views and ideas are heard in society.

Communication is more than a simple exchange of messages and signals. And true freedom of speech depends on every member of society being able to communicate with whoever he or she wishes.

People in a pub have a lively exchange of views using sign language.

Date: **February 1996**
Place: **Denmark**
Issue: **Free to spread hatred?**

An extreme, racist political party in Denmark, the neo-Nazi DNSB (Danish National Socialist Movement), opened its own radio station, Oasis, in February 1996. The authorities gave it permission to broadcast twice a week, provided it did not break any of the country's strict laws against racism.

The chairman of the DNSB, Jonni Hansen, welcomed the decision to allow the broadcasting to go ahead, but admitted that if he ever gained power he would not allow any groups opposing his views to broadcast and would put an end to freedom of speech.

Placing limits

In allowing the DNSB to broadcast, the Danish government is respecting the group's right to express its opinions. However, Danish law limits what the group can say. The DNSB promotes racist politics that many people consider offensive and unacceptable. Inciting racial hatred can create tensions within multicultural communities and possibly lead to violence, so, like the Danish, most countries have laws against it. But these laws, by their very nature, place limits on free speech.

Living together

In any school there are children and teachers with all kinds of ideas and viewpoints. They may have various interests and hobbies, or different ideas about what the school rules should be. Some children may eat meat and others may be vegetarians. Some may follow different religions or come from very different family backgrounds.

In the same way the society we live in is made up of a multitude

German protesters carry a banner at an anti-Nazi demonstration in Berlin. It shows the Nazi symbol, the swastika, being smashed. Should free speech be granted to people, such as the Nazis, who preach hatred of other people?

of individuals and groups. They may have different political or religious views, different ideas about how people should behave, or different tastes in art or music. In a society where there is freedom of speech, all these people should be allowed to express their points of view. And most of the time all their views can be expressed without any problem or conflict. But what happens when the interests of the different individuals or groups do clash violently with each other or with society as a whole? Are there limits to freedom of speech? Is it acceptable to allow free speech to those who would deny it to others?

A new Hindu temple rises above the roofs of Neasden in London, England. For many, the temple symbolizes how religions can live successfully side by side.

An impossible ideal?

No society has ever managed to allow complete freedom of speech for all its citizens. Countries such as the United States or Australia may be considered democracies, but their governments still place careful limits on what their citizens can say. If the rights of one individual or group are to be protected, then the rights of another will probably have to be limited in some way. Most public debate about freedom of speech revolves around how severe these limits should be and to which areas they should apply, rather than whether they should exist at all.

'a multitude of individuals'

In the classroom, as in society as a whole, people have different views and ideas. School gives them a chance to discuss and share them.

A framework of law

Society, with all its conflicting stresses and strains, is held together by the framework of laws passed by government. As in the example opposite, it may be illegal for groups to incite hatred or violence. Such laws are often employed to control racist abuse. Many countries have laws aimed at stopping racist abuse in the classroom or the workplace, so that people can communicate freely without being threatened or bullied. Books which put forward racist views may be taken off the shelves of libraries.

Over 85 countries have now signed the 1976 International Covenant on Civil and Political Rights, a treaty which includes limits to free expression when that encourages national, racial or religious hatred.

19

Libel laws

Most people believe that telling damaging lies about someone else is an abuse of freedom of speech, so laws may be passed to protect individuals against slander and libel. Slander is untrue speech that is intended to damage someone else's reputation, and libel is the publication of written words or of pictures which do the same.

Many laws are designed to protect the rights of individuals. Medical records, which are confidential, are often kept on file in computer systems. Few people would want such information to be freely available to the public. Data protection laws, first introduced in West Germany and Scandinavia in the 1970s, give individuals the right to check on the information being held about them.

Parliaments around the world, such as Congress in the USA, try to frame laws that are in the public good.

'an abuse of freedom of speech'

Date: 1994-95
Place: United States of America
Issue: What is a suitable book?

On over 450 occasions in 1994-95 campaigning groups in the United States tried to have particular books banned from school lessons or from public libraries, claiming they were acting 'in the public good' because the books were unsuitable.

The reasons for these challenges varied in different states and cities. Religious groups complained that some books contained bad language or described immoral behaviour. Some people complained that sex education books were not suitable for young children. Anti-racist groups complained that some books were insulting to ethnic groups living in the United States. Others demanded that books should show a more positive attitude towards women.

The campaigning groups were successful in 169 cases. The author whose works were challenged the most was the very popular children's writer Judy Blume. The reason? The campaigners complained that her books were too open about subjects teenagers found interesting, such as sex.

Should governments step in?

Governments are often faced with a dilemma. How much should they try to regulate the organizations controlling communications, such as publishers, broadcasters, advertisers, religious or political movements, local councils or big companies? On the one hand, governments may not wish to pass too many laws regulating these bodies. They may support the idea of a free press, where both sides of an argument can be heard and debated. On the other hand, they may feel that some of these organizations are abusing their freedom and not acting in the public interest.

Protecting the individual

One of the hottest debates about press freedom concerns individual privacy. The press may harass people in the news, making their lives a misery. The right of reporters to investigate and the public to know must be balanced by the individual's right to privacy. Whilst libel and slander laws stop the press from publishing outright lies, it is harder to frame laws that protect privacy without also limiting press freedom. Instead of specific laws, many countries encourage the media to regulate themselves, with codes of practice and guidelines for journalists and editors to follow. In the UK, there is a Press Complaints Authority, an independent body to which people can complain if they feel someone has not complied with these codes of practice.

In the public good

Every government has a responsibility to draw up laws which are fair, offering protection to the greatest possible number of its citizens. In the same way each citizen has a responsibility to treat other citizens fairly, without threats or abuse. Freedom of speech is not just about putting across one's own point of view, it also means listening to other people's arguments and trying to understand them. Limiting freedom of speech or expression is often justified by governments and individuals as being in the public interest, or for the good of the public. But there are many issues, such as what is a 'suitable' book, where views about what is in the 'public good' may differ. Sometimes it is not just governments but individuals who have to decide for themselves.

Some press photographers spend much of their time hunting down celebrities to snap.

Date: 1995
Place: Canada
Issue: Freedom to advertise

In September 1995 the Canadian Supreme Court ruled that the 1988 Tobacco Products Control Act was against the Canadian constitution, because it denied freedom of speech to the companies manufacturing cigarettes. Despite this, the Canadian government continued in 1996 to draw up plans banning cigarette advertising and sponsorship of public events by the tobacco industry. The government's aim was to protect the public from the illnesses associated with smoking, such as heart disease and lung cancer.

In a family, parents make most of the rules although children may have a say as well. But is this a fair balance? And at what age should children begin to control their own lives?

Many people choose to smoke even though they know about the health dangers. Does cigarette advertising encourage people in this choice?

resources, can put considerable pressure on the government as well. A democratic government has to respond to its people's wishes but there are many viewpoints to consider.

Do adults know best?

The debate about free and fair communication affects many sections of society. For example, children are often abused and their rights certainly need protecting. But how much freedom should children have in turn? Should they be free to express their views and make their own decisions? Many people would say that adults do know what is best for children, who have not yet had enough experience to make decisions that are sensible and safe.

Pressure from the public

Censorship 'in the public interest' takes many forms. It may be carried out not only by the government, but by all kinds of organizations or companies which control the media. It is often demanded by groups campaigning for human rights. It is mainly as a result of pressure from campaigning groups that the Canadian government has continued with their plans to ban cigarette advertising. The cigarette manufacturers, with their large financial

Date: 1996
Place: Egypt
Issue: Women and censorship

On 18 January 1996 Egyptian actresses called a press conference complaining that they were subject of attacks in the popular press. They had been called irreligious for appearing in films and magazines when not wearing the face veil and other forms of dress demanded by many Muslims. Particular anger in the press was directed at *The Immigrant*, a film by Youssef Chahine which starred the actress Yousra. The actresses at the conference said that the real reason Yousra was being criticized was that she was a successful woman in a society dominated by men.

Women in films, such as the Indian one above, provoke fierce debate, particularly in strongly religious countries, about how women should be represented. Strict Muslim dress codes are equally controversial. Many Muslim women believe the veil they wear gives them the freedom to avoid harassment by men.

'Women often suffer abuse from men'

A woman's place

The rights of women are also fiercely debated around the world. Does society have a duty to protect the right of women to communicate freely and to be treated fairly by the media? Women often suffer abuse from men if they speak their minds. In many countries women have few rights. They may be stopped from organizing politically and expressing their views.

The Western news media often report how women are dressed or look, rather than what they actually have to say. They do not treat men in the same way. Many women believe that such reporting should be stopped. Others say that too many controls might harm the cause of women, as journalists might not write about women's issues at all to avoid any difficulties in the way they are represented.

Date:
1988
Place:
United Kingdom
Issue:
Gay rights and
censorship

In May 1988 the UK parliament passed a law making it illegal for local councils to teach that a homosexual couple could be an acceptable family relationship. On 23 September 1988 a play called *Trapped in Time*, due to be performed in a school by the Avon Touring Theatre Company, was banned by the headmaster because it included a scene in which someone explained how he was gay. The headmaster was afraid of breaking the new law.

Making a statement: gays and lesbians march through San Francisco, in the American state of California, in 1990. The march is a yearly event aiming to bring the issues that surround homosexuality to public attention. In some countries, gay men and lesbians are not able to communicate freely or demonstrate in this way.

The right to be different

In many countries, people are not free to express their true sexual feelings for one another. Homosexual relationships may be illegal, and gay writing or films may be censored. As in the UK, it may be illegal for teachers to promote homosexuality as a 'normal' way of life. Among the countries in which homosexuality is completely banned and actively repressed are Iran, Ecuador, Algeria, Botswana and Romania.

Laws can work for or against such minority groups. They may limit the ways in which sexuality can be shown or expressed, but equally laws may protect the right of individuals to express their sexuality as they please.

'laws can work for or against minority groups'

Pornography

Pornography is regarded as a threat to sections of society, especially children, so there are restrictions on the sale of pornographic material. Many governments, local councils and media organizations take action against images, words or pop songs that they believe to be obscene to protect the public from indecent words and images.

24

But deciding what is decent and what is not is a very difficult task. Standards vary from one country to another, from one part of society to another and from one person to another. Arguments arise over how far the public needs protecting. Does pornography encourage people to be immoral? Experts cannot agree just how it affects people.

Violence

Violence is a subject which arouses even more debate. Do violent films and videos encourage people to behave violently? Many people believe they do. They say that some children or adults will copy violent heroes they have seen on screen. As a result they should be

The singer Madonna's videos have been criticized as pornographic and blasphemous. She claims she is challenging conventions, others say she shocks for the sake of publicity.

prevented from seeing them – to protect the public from crimes such as murder. Others claim that it has never actually been proved that people get the idea for their crimes from films and videos.

An electronic gadget called a 'V-chip' (V is for violence) can be built into television sets. It helps parents black out any programmes which are rated as too violent for children. However some parents say that there is already a perfectly good control – the off-switch. People who argue against censorship of violent or sexually explicit material often highlight the importance of individual choice: it is up to us to select and control what we see or read, not governments.

The video of the violent film Robocop was seen by many children.

A picture of society

Do artists and writers have a duty to reflect what is happening in society, even if it is unpleasant or violent? Or would they improve and inspire people more by only showing the most positive sides of human nature? Perhaps the greatest artists are the ones who show the full range of human experience. They force us to question what is right and good.

Religious expression

Some of the fiercest debates about free expression concern religious beliefs. Religious free expression includes the right to worship, to preach to others and to read and distribute holy books or scriptures. Throughout history there has been strife and warfare in the name of religion. Sometimes violent clashes have been part of wider political problems, as in the Middle East. Some people believe that all religions are different paths to the same truth. But others believe that they alone follow the true faith and they may think that it is their god-given duty to prevent people from holding other views.

'in the name of religion'

Strong beliefs

Many of the strongest calls to limit religious expression come from fundamentalists, who believe that every word of their scriptures is literally true. Christian fundamentalists, for example, may call for censorship of school books, films and videos. In the United States some Christians believe that schools should not be allowed to teach the theory of evolution, which suggests that the living things on Earth developed very slowly over many millions of years. Instead, they believe that the words of the Bible, which says that God created the Earth and everything on it, should be taught.

A Baptist church in Tennessee. Tennessee has a strong Christian tradition and feelings run very high against the teaching of evolutionary theory.

Date:
1993
Place:
Bangladesh
Issue:
Blasphemous
writing

In 1993 a novel called *Shame* was banned in Bangladesh. Its author was a woman doctor named Taslima Nasreen (pictured below). Her views were said to be blasphemous, insulting to the faith of Islam.

Bangladeshi religious leaders claimed that Taslima was plotting against their beliefs and issued a fatwah or ruling saying that she should be killed. There were public demonstrations of hatred against her and she was forced to go into hiding.

On 10 August 1994 Taslima was finally forced to flee from Bangladesh and go to live far away in Sweden.

Minds of our own

The conflicting views within society about morality, sexuality, religious beliefs and other issues are part of the richness and strength of civilization. There is a lot of truth in the common saying that 'it would be a very boring world if we all agreed with each other'.

The most difficult question of all is who should decide? Who should draw up the rules? For it could be argued that it is up to each individual to make up his or her own mind about what is moral and good and what is not, and leave it to others to make up their minds for themselves.

(Above) British author Salman Rushdie was sentenced to death by an Iranian fatwah for writing a book, The Satanic Verses, which many Muslims found blasphemous. This 1989 demonstration in London supported the fatwah.

(Right) The rap-star Ice-T raised a storm of argument in 1992 with his violent song 'Cop Killer'. It was removed from his album in the USA, banned in Ireland and cut from live shows in Australia. Should his fans have had a say in these decisions?

Laws to protect religion

Most countries have laws against blasphemy, the insulting of God, but their importance varies, often depending on the links between religious leaders and the government in power. Bangladesh is a strongly Muslim country. Although its government does not actively support the fatwah (a ruling on religious matters), it has done nothing to protect Taslima Nasreen. In Iran, the Muslim government has actively supported a similar fatwah issued against the British author Salman Rushdie.

Within one country people may follow several different religions, so it is especially important that everyone has the right to express their religious beliefs freely. But it is also important that they do not force their own religious beliefs upon other people.

Date: 28 August 1963
Place: Washington DC, USA
Issue: Speaking up for change

On 28 August 1963, over 250,000 people marched on the US capital, Washington DC, to demonstrate against racial discrimination. At the rally at the end of the march, the crowds of demonstrators heard perhaps one of the most famous political speeches of all time. It was given by Martin Luther King (below) and was an impassioned plea for African-Americans to be given the same civil and political rights as white Americans. 'I have a dream' he said repeatedly throughout. His dream was one of equality.

The march and speech were the culmination of years of protest against the unequal treatment of African-Americans in the United States. The government had promised reforms but had been slow to bring in new laws. In the face of such huge public outcry and the inspiring words of Martin Luther King, the government finally moved. The first Civil Rights Act of 1964 forbade discrimination on the grounds of race in the use of most public facilities.

The US government had at last recognized the need for equal rights for all its citizens.

Free speech and politics

Major protest movements like the American Civil Rights movement put sustained pressure on the government of the day to change or reform its policies. One of the most important reasons for freedom of speech is to ensure that protest can be heard and acted upon. Similarly, the public has a right to know what governments are doing and hold them accountable for their actions.

'accountable for their actions'

In a country where there is free speech, one of the principal concerns of the media is how the country is governed. Newspaper articles, television documentaries and even satirical comedy programmes constantly scrutinize the government, question its policies and criticize or praise the results of its actions. In the same way that the media shapes people's moral and personal views, it also profoundly influences their political ideas and opinions.

In 1968, Martin Luther King was silenced by an assassin's gun. His words live on.

Date: 1993
Place: Germany
Issue: Insulting political leaders

A German pop group Die Ärzte wrote a song called 'Helmut Kohl Beats his Wife'. Helmut Kohl was the German Chancellor. The words of the song were intended to shock rather than to make a serious political point, but in 1993 the group's recording company refused to release the song. Die Ärzte therefore released the record themselves and it did well.

At a concert in Munich they were told that if they sang the song they would be arrested by the police. The group obeyed, playing only the music – but the audience sang the forbidden words.

This puppet from the British TV programme *Spitting Image* makes fun of Helmut Kohl. Is such mockery in the public interest, cutting politicians down to size? Or does such lack of respect undermine the political process?

Going too far?

Sometimes politicians feel that the process of questioning goes too far, that the media move beyond political issues to personal insults. Comedy programmes such as British-produced *Spitting Image* are sometimes criticized for this, as was the song by Die Ärzte. Other people argue that, by the nature of their work, politicians choose to expose themselves to the public eye so they must accept bad press alongside more positive reporting.

Similarly, people argue about how much a politician's private life should be examined. How far do private matters affect their work? François Mitterrand (inset) was President of France from 1981 to 1995. When he first ran for the presidency Mitterrand knew he was suffering from cancer, but his doctor was forbidden from informing the press. Was the right of the public to know if their president could do his job properly really outweighed by the president's right to privacy?

29

People who argue against any control of this sort of information say that the public do have a right to know – that if they are to form opinions and reach decisions about how to vote, they must be possession of the necessary facts. But what are the *necessary* facts?

Controlling information

In the process of running a country, governments accumulate vast amounts of information. The information ranges from individual medical records and population surveys to the results of scientific research and matters concerned with the country's defence against attack from other states. Sometimes, governments may claim that it is in the public interest to conceal much of this information. For example during a war governments want to ensure that valuable information does not reach the enemy. In this case official secrecy may be used to protect the lives of both soldiers in action and citizens at home. Letters written home from the battlefield may be heavily censored.

A British World War II poster warns people to think before they speak. An enemy agent might overhear them and find out information about British battle plans and troop movements.

During the 1960s and 70s people all around the world protested against America's war in Vietnam. They had seen terrible pictures of the war on television.

Managing the news

In the 1960s the United States fought a war against Vietnam, in South-East Asia. When uncensored pictures of the war were broadcast on American television it brought home to viewers the horrors of war, and many Americans turned against the government and the war. There were public protests and by 1975 the US government had decided to stop the fighting.

In 1990-91, in the Gulf War, the US and its European and Gulf allies fought Iraq, after Iraqi troops had invaded Kuwait. Television reports of the war shown in the US and Europe concentrated on the

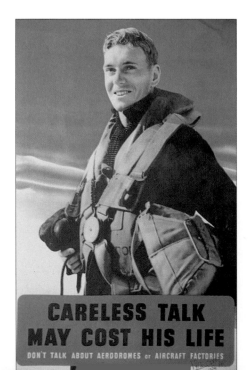

technology of the weapons used, rather than on the people who were killed and the cities which were bombed. Americans protesting against this war complained that their rallies received only one per cent of the total news coverage. The authorities had learned the lesson of Vietnam. They presented the Gulf War as 'clean' and so retained the support of the American people. But was this really in the public interest?

CARELESS TALK MAY COST HIS LIFE

DON'T TALK ABOUT AERODROMES or AIRCRAFT FACTORIES

While governments may claim to use such official secrecy in the public interest, they may really be acting to cover up mistakes they have made or to put out political propaganda or lies. Members of the public have to decide for themselves whether their government really is speaking truthfully when it says it is acting in the public interest. In some countries, such as the United States, laws guarantee a certain amount of freedom of information.

'what are the necessary facts?'

The United States National Archives has hundreds of millions of documents which are 'classified' – they are secret and can only be seen by people approved by the security service. Hundreds of millions more are held by the Central Intelligence Agency and by the Pentagon, the US military headquarters. In November 1994 American President Bill Clinton ordered 44 million National Archives documents to be 'declassified' – taken off the secret list.

Date: 1988
Place: UK
Issue: Whose voice?

For many years British governments had looked for ways of censoring statements by Sinn Fein, a Northern Ireland political party closely associated with the Provisional IRA, a terrorist organization. Prime Minister Margaret Thatcher wished to put a stop to the 'oxygen of publicity'. She believed that it was not in the public interest to broadcast interviews with Sinn Fein leaders. In 1988 these were banned, but many questioned the effectiveness of the policy because actors were allowed to read the words spoken during the interview. The ban was lifted in 1994.

An actor reads the words of Gerry Adams, after the British ban on broadcasting the voices of Sinn Fein leaders.

Controlling terrorism

As with war, similar arguments arise in government policy on terrorism, which may also threaten national security. Sometimes media interviews with terrorists are banned to stop them receiving publicity. Governments may do this to protect the public from bombs and hijackings. Even when the intentions of such censorship are good, there is a danger that, by limiting the right of terrorists to express their views, a government may seem to be acting undemocratically and so play into the terrorists' hands.

Big business

One of the major concerns of any government is that the economy of its country is successful. As a result, big businesses have considerable influence on government decisions.

Sometimes government has information that, if made public, could damage a business and so the economy. It must decide if it is in the public interest to give out this information or whether it is better to keep it quiet. And if the government does not tell the public of its decision, how is anyone going to question it?

The Shell Oil company has built oil rigs in Ogoniland in south-east Nigeria. Local people have protested that their land has been polluted and that they have no share of the huge wealth brought by the oil. Their protests have been broken up by government forces and a number of people killed.

Corruption

Sometimes, politicians accept money from the business world in return for suppressing information or adjusting it. There are examples of this sort of bribery and corruption in the history of most countries. However, today, the problem is often bad in the developing world, where the laws and checks against corruption are rarely acted on.

If a poor country has a resource, such as gold or oil, that is in international demand it is easy to see how corruption and abuse can occur. International companies competing to exploit the resource can bribe politicians and buy off opponents. In the same way governments may only allow companies to operate in return for large sums paid to their political party or into secret bank accounts. And then, if something does go wrong, it may be difficult for ordinary people to find out the facts. In Nigeria, the government has suppressed environmental protests by some of its people against the oil industry, which provides the country with its main source of wealth.

Date: 1994
Place: Italy
Issue: Business influence in politics

Silvio Berlusconi is a leading Italian businessman. In 1994, he formed a new political party, Forza Italia, to contest the general election that year. With only two months' campaigning, his party won the most number of seats in the Italian parliament and Berlusconi became prime minister.

Many people were concerned about Berlusconi's victory. His main business interests were in commercial television and some people suggested he had promoted his party through the TV channels he controlled. After his victory he was accused of using his media power to promote his government's policies. Allegations of corruption followed and Berlusconi was forced to resign.

Silvio Berlusconi campaigns in Naples, Italy. The media tycoon won the Italian general election for Forza Italia in March 1994, but was forced out of office in December that same year.

Prime time politics

Big business and politics can be a dangerous combination, especially where freedom of speech is concerned. Big companies may interfere in a country's politics, trying to use their power to influence a government's policies. Because Silvio Berlusconi owned the most popular television channels it was difficult for other candidates to get their messages across to the voters. In most countries there are laws which give political parties 'equal air time' to broadcast their ideas.

Staying in power

All governments, whether they are elected or have taken power by force, need the media if they want to stay in power – to 'sell' their policies to the people. With a free press, this may mean spending time and effort to present their ideas in a way that the media will report favourably. In the lead up to a general election, all the political parties campaign throughout the media to attract people's votes. But for some governments the temptation is to use their power to control the press completely – to cease to have free speech and to operate a system of extreme censorship.

CENSORSHIP IN ACTION

Date: January 1996
Place: Croatia
Issue: Government control of the media

In 1992, following the break-up of Yugoslavia, Croatia was recognized as an independent nation.

On 15 January 1996 the Croatian president, Franjo Tudjman, made an important speech to parliament. He called for greater regulation of the media, claiming that democratic rights had been abused and that 'the freedom of journalistic activity had not been coordinated with the necessity to provide legal protection for citizens as individuals, companies and state interests'.

Three days later the government closed down an independent radio station called LAE and gave its broadcasting licence to someone who was a member of HDZ, the ruling political party. And on 1 February the Croatian parliament voted to replace the director of the national Croatian radio and TV with another HDZ party member.

A Croatian soldier stands guard. In the 1990s, free speech has been severely challenged during the wars which tore the former Republic of Yugoslavia apart.

Power and control

Why does anyone want to limit free speech? Communication is very powerful. Television images, newspaper articles and advertisements can all change the way people see the world. That is why, during a revolution or war, soldiers try to capture the main radio or television station before any other building. They, or those giving them orders, wish to control the supply of information.

'why does anyone want to limit free speech?'

Any kind of interference with free communication, especially by official bodies, is an example of censorship. It is nothing new and, as we have seen, can be desirable. The word censor was first used by the ancient Romans, as early as 443 BC. Throughout history, kings, queens, priests, generals and governments have used censorship to maintain their power and control. During the Middle Ages in Europe the Christian Church censored books and tortured and burnt alive many people found guilty of spreading what the Church authorities claimed were false beliefs, or heresies.

Date:
1632
Place:
Rome
Issue:

Religion versus science

The Roman Catholic Church was very powerful in Europe in the 1600s. In 1632 its leader, Pope Urban VIII, brought the Italian scientist Galileo Galilei to trial in Rome. Galileo had described in a book how the planet Earth travelled around the Sun, but the Pope disagreed with his theory and placed Galileo under house arrest. His books were banned and his letters were censored.

It was not until 1992 that the Pope, John Paul II, admitted that Galileo had been correct.

Moves against censorship

When printing became widespread in the 1600s and 1700s, leaflets and books reached more and more people. Political and religious views spread like wildfire. Rulers and governments banned many books and stopped plays from being performed, but there was increasing resistance to this type of control. In 1775, European settlers in America rebelled against British rule to form the independent United States with their own bill of rights. At much the same time, the French Revolution of 1789 destroyed the old order, the French king was beheaded and a new system of government proclaimed, in which individual rights were to be respected.

The Tree of Liberty, symbol of the French Revolution of 1789. It was during this period that people began demanding their right to free speech. However, the revolutionaries soon censored their opponents every bit as ruthlessly as the royalists had before them.

Dictators and totalitarian states

People's increased awareness of their rights did not stop censorship. Indeed, as the technology of communication improved in the 19th and early 20th centuries, with the addition of radio and film, governments began to recognize more and more the power of the media. In the 1930s in Germany the Nazi government led by Adolf Hitler banned music, pictures and books that were not in line with government beliefs and Joseph Stalin introduced similar bans in the Soviet Union throughout the 1930s and 40s.

Science is silenced by religion, as Galileo stands trial before Pope Urban VIII in 1632.

Young Nazis in the Hitler Youth group burn books at Salzburg in Austria in 1938. The Nazis banned books by Jews and other ethnic groups as well as many political books which did not support Nazi ideas and policies.

Both Hitler and Stalin are often described as dictators: they had almost total control of their governments and they expected the orders they gave, or dictated, to be automatically carried out. They ruled through the political party they led, the Nazi party in Germany and the Communist party in the Soviet Union. All other political parties were banned. A country ruled in this way is called a totalitarian state. Such states by their very nature suppress free speech. Often they have opponents jailed and murdered. The Irish playwright and author George Bernard Shaw (1856-1950) once described assassination (political murder) as an extreme form of censorship.

Propaganda

Totalitarian states do not just censor opposition to their rule, they also use the media to promote their rule. This sort of political presentation is called propaganda. Most governments use propaganda of some form or another, but in totalitarian states, where no other group has a voice, propaganda becomes an essential part of government control. In the Soviet Union, posters promoted the Communist party and newspapers celebrated its achievements. Similar methods were used in Nazi Germany – even book burnings were turned into celebrations of Nazism.

Racist censorship

The Nazi government also used censorship and propaganda to carry out anti-Jewish policies. They blamed the Jews for many of Germany's economic and social problems. Many governments throughout history have passed laws which prevent racial minorities from expressing themselves freely. In the worst cases, whole cultures have been destroyed and peoples murdered. This is called genocide. It is what ultimately happened to the Jewish community in Germany.

In the early 1990s war swept through the countries of former

This Soviet poster of 1939 celebrates the fight against the Nazis. However, under Stalin, the Soviet Union maintained just as tight a control of the media as the Nazis.

Yugoslavia and many thousands of innocent people were imprisoned or killed just because they belonged to the 'wrong' ethnic group. Propaganda was at work here, too, with leaders justifying their actions on the grounds of 'ethnic cleansing'.

'ethnic cleansing'

A woman places flowers on a grave in Bosnia during the 1990s civil war. This conflict grew out of bitter divisions between Bosnian Serbs, Bosnian Croats and Bosnian Muslims. It gave rise to a chilling new term: 'ethnic cleansing'.

Date:
February 1996
Place:
Philippines
Issue:
Silencing a journalist

On 12 February 1996 Fernando Reyes was working in his office in Dipolog City in the Philippines. He was well-known as a lawyer who worked for human rights causes. As editor of a publication called *Press Freedom*, he was a fearless critic of the army and of corrupt politicians. Because of this, he sometimes received death threats. But, on 12 February, it was not an empty threat. A man burst into the building and shot Fernando Reyes dead.

The intruder ran from the office and escaped on a motorcycle. No one has been charged with the murder.

New methods

Today, new technical developments, such as satellite television which can be beamed across national borders, have made it harder for governments to control communications. However they have not given up trying: they may jam broadcasts, sending out radio signals that make it impossible to pick up a programme. They may bring in strict laws controlling the press, with heavy fines, imprisonment or even execution for those who break the rules. Reporters who ask too many questions may find themselves sacked or jailed. In March 1996 a report by the Committee to Protect Journalists claimed that 182 journalists had been imprisoned around the world during the previous year.

Date:
1983, 1989
Place:
Romania
Issue:
Keeping control of information

From1965 Romania was ruled by a dictator called Nicolae Ceaucescu. He claimed to be a communist, but was really only interested in personal power. In the 1980s people began to protest against years of oppression and poor living standards. In a last-ditch attempt to keep control and stop opposition groups publishing information about the corruption and inefficiency of the regime, the Romanian government forced every owner of a typewriter or photocopier to register them with the authorities. In that way the authorities hoped to be able to trace the source of any anti-government publication. It did not work. The regime was overthrown in 1989.

Do-it-yourself media

Romania is not the only example of such restrictive government measures. In China, in 1989, after hundreds of unarmed students confronted and were then killed by government troops in Beijing, Chinese soldiers tried to prevent the many faxes from all over the world protesting about the massacre being received on Chinese fax machines.

The pro-democracy demonstrations in Beijing in China in 1989 were ruthlessly suppressed by the Chinese army.

Over the years, new developments in the media, such as photocopiers, faxes, desktop publishing and the internet have enabled writers to produce and distribute their own material. Lack of control over these do-it-yourself media worries even less repressive governments.

Internet international

The internet is the largest and least controlled do-it-yourself medium of communication to have grown up in recent years. This international computer network may be operated by individuals around the world. It by-passes publishers, media owners and national authorities, and so many people see it as a new form of democratic expression.

Others, however, worry that the internet may aid the spread of pornography or of terrorist

The revolution in Romania of 1989 was a violent one. Ceaucescu was overthrown and killed.

An abandoned kindergarten at Pirki, just 20 kilometres from Chernobyl in Ukraine after the 1986 nuclear accident. Ukraine was then part of the Soviet Union, and the government tried to hush up news of the disaster. Its after-effects are still felt in the area.

activity, because information about bomb-making can be found on it. In 1996 many governments, including those of the United States, Germany, Thailand, Singapore and Australia, began to look into ways that the internet could be censored and controlled with new laws.

History with a difference

In many countries, political censorship is common in the classroom. The authorities may tell teachers what lessons they have to teach. For example, there may be just one official version of history. Governments may order the rewriting of history books, so that only people of whom they approve appear as heroes, or their country's role is seen in a good light. In Japan, school history books make almost no mention of Japanese aggression towards neighbouring states in the first part of the 20th century.

Silence is golden...?

Governments may sometimes abuse the laws on official secrecy (see page 30). They may sometimes refuse to tell the public just how many people die of hunger or disease or accidents at work or how badly land is polluted. If they tell the truth about these things it might create a bad impression abroad, and stop foreign companies opening factories there. The truth may cause panic amongst the population, or show up the politicians' incompetence or corruption.

When the nuclear plant at Chernobyl in the former Soviet Union exploded in 1986 the rest of the world only knew about it because a monitoring station in Sweden registered a sudden and excessive increase in radiation. But even then the Soviet government played down the scale of the disaster, deceiving not only the international community but its own people, too.

Date:
February 1996
Place:
Guatemala
Issue:
Free speech in
the workplace

Both Débora Guzmán Chupén and her husband Félix González are trade unionists working in the clothing industry in Guatemala. On 12 February 1996 Débora opened her mail and found an unsigned letter threatening her life. It was one of many death threats she and Félix had received. A year before, she had been kidnapped and warned that she would be killed unless she and her husband stopped organizing trade union activities.

Places of work, such as factories, can be dangerous. Organizations like trade unions demand better safety standards at work but some employers do not want to hear their views. They do not want to meet the extra costs that improved safety may bring.

Trade unions

Trade unions aim to protect workers' rights and to campaign for fair wages. Working people need to communicate freely with each other and with the public if they are to form a trade union. Some governments and companies regard unions as a threat. Although trade unions are perfectly legal in many countries, in others they are banned or else they may be allowed in theory, but belonging to them is made very difficult. There are no trade unions in, for example, Saudi Arabia, Myanmar (Burma) or Cambodia.

Blowing the whistle

Workers who report the illegal or dangerous activities of their bosses are called whistle-blowers. In some countries, such as the United States and Sweden, there are now laws to protect whistle-blowers. But elsewhere they may be sacked and unable to find other work because no one will employ them. In some countries they risk being beaten up or even murdered. Corrupt governments and police turn a blind eye to these activities. The money made by the business world brings its own powers of censorship.

Japanese workers on strike in 1989. Sometimes employees feel that striking is the only way to get their message across to the management. But in many cases it is illegal for them to do so.

MAKING A STAND

Date:
December 1995
Place:
Myanmar (Burma)
Issue:
Standing up for
freedom of
speech

U Sein Hla Aung was surprised to be arrested on 16 December 1995 for distributing videos. After all, these were not illegal copies of the latest films, just pictures of the political debates and gatherings held outside the house of a woman called Aung San Suu Kyi.

Aung San Suu Kyi is a political leader in Myanmar (Burma). In the 1980s she campaigned against the military rulers of her country, demanding democracy and basic human rights. Thousands of her supporters were arrested or killed.

'her supporters were arrested or killed'

In 1990 Aung San Suu Kyi's party won 81 per cent of the seats at the general election. But instead of handing over power to her, as they were supposed to do, the generals heading the military government placed her under house arrest. In the following year she was awarded the Nobel Peace Prize, but despite this international honour she was not released from arrest until July 1995. It was then that she began to hold gatherings outside her home. In January 1996 members of a group of dancers, singers and comedians who had performed there were arrested.

The press around the world has reported the story of Aung San Suu Kyi, but journalists from her own country have been put in jail.

Democracy campaigner Aung San Suu Kyi comes to the gate of her home to address her supporters in 1995, although she has already been under house arrest for expressing her views. Standing up for free speech often requires bravery and perseverance.

News vendors sell papers on the streets in Shenzhen in southern China. The Chinese government, like many others, places strict controls on the press. Despite this, people continue to fight for greater freedom, both inside and outside China.

Indian villagers gather to watch a TV set. Modern media command great power and influence. They can be used to educate and entertain, or they can be used to confuse and mislead.

Is freedom of speech really such an important issue? If you were starving to death, would you care how the story was reported? Or if your life was threatened would you continue to speak out?

In prison for their beliefs

All over the world there are prisoners of conscience, nobody knows how many. As you read this book, many thousands of them are being tortured or kept in jail simply for speaking their mind, talking at political meetings, writing books or making films. Some of them will be executed.

Even where free speech carries extreme penalties, many people still speak out bravely, risking prison or execution. International monitoring of human rights is very important. Organizations such as Amnesty International work on behalf of prisoners of conscience, making sure that they are not forgotten by the world.

Date:
1995
Place:
Ivory Coast
Issue:
Jailing
dissidents

On 28 December 1995 Emmanuel Kore, a journalist working on a publication called *La Voie*, was sent to prison for two years and fined US$6000. Abou Drahamne Sangare, head of the Nouvel Horizon publishing group and deputy leader of an opposition party called the Ivorian Popular Front, was also jailed. Another journalist, Freedom Neruda, was also jailed for two years on 11 January 1996, and publication of *La Voie* was suspended for three months.

Free speech campaigns

There are many different groups around the world which campaign about censorship, press freedom, artistic freedom, human rights and religious beliefs. There are journalists' and writers' unions, political parties, language campaigns and pressure groups.

All these groups may ask governments to pass laws which respect human rights, or to use their power and influence to get other governments to take action. To this end, it is useful to have official declarations of human rights so that everybody understands just what they mean. Not only the United Nations, but continental and regional organizations in Europe, Africa and North America, as well as many individual countries have drawn up declarations of citizens' rights.

A protestor waves a flag during the 1989 Romanian revolution. The hated badge of the government has been cut from the centre of the flag.

Raise your voices!

As an individual you can help organize events that support these groups. Freedom of speech is an issue that affects every one of us. Perhaps the most important thing any one person can do is to keep talking, discussing what is going on in the world and speaking out, listening to the arguments of other people and learning. We all have to stand up for our rights and to be aware of the rights of others. In the words of Victor Jara, a poet and song-writer in Chile, who was secretly executed after a right-wing military coup in 1973:

I learned the language of my masters and bosses.
They killed me over and over for daring to raise my voice.
But I get up off the ground again helped by the
hands of others.
For now I'm not alone, now there are
many of us.

'freedom of speech is an issue that affects every one of us'

Glossary

bill of rights: laws or guidelines which set out the rights of citizens within a state.

blasphemy: contempt or insults offered to God. Blasphemy can be anything from using God's name as a swear word to criticizing or making fun of religious ideas. People have very different views as to what is or is not blasphemous.

Braille: raised dots used to represent words on a page, which can be felt by a blind person.

censorship: the act of censoring, that is stopping information or ideas that may be considered harmful or politically dangerous from being communicated through any medium to a wider audience or public.

Christianity: the world religion founded about 2000 years ago by Jesus of Nazareth; its followers are called Christians. There are many different branches of Christianity.

Civil Rights Movement: the name given in the USA to the long campaign by certain groups and individuals to gain equal rights for the African-American population. The campaign was most active during the 1950s and 1960s.

Communist: describes the political belief and movement of Communism, which aims to establish a community where there is no private ownership and each member works for the common benefit. The former Soviet Union was a Communist state.

constitution: (in the context of this book) the system of laws and rights established by a state which provide the framework in which each government can operate.

Convention on the Rights of the Child: an international treaty made by the United Nations in 1989 stating the freedoms and provisions that all children should have, such as the freedom from abuse and the right to good healthcare and education.

degrade: to take away dignity or value, to bring into contempt.

democracy: a system of government by the population of a state, usually through elected representatives.

desktop publishing: the use of a computer programme to produce and publish material.

dictatorship: a state or country that is ruled by a dictator, an individual leader who has complete power, rather than sharing power with a government or parliament.

discrimination: the act of choosing one thing rather than another; in the world of rights, discrimination is usually used as a term to describe treating or judging someone unfairly because of who they are or what they look like.

economics: the way in which money and resources are managed.

e-mail (electronic mail): a way of using telephone lines to send messages from one computer to another.

expurgation: cutting out parts of a book which are thought to be indecent, cleaning up.

fax (facsimile): a way of sending a copy of a document, letter or visual image via a telephone line.

freedom of information: the right of the public to find out information held by the authorities.

freedom of speech: the ability to communicate or express oneself freely.

heresy: a belief which goes against the agreed teachings of a religion.

house arrest: being forbidden to leave one's home.

impart: to give out or share ideas or information.

immoral: offending ideas of what is right or decent.

intolerance: refusal to put up with other people's views or behaviour.

internet: a worldwide computer communications network.

Islam: the world religion founded by the Prophet Muhammad in AD 622. Its holy book is the Qur'an and its followers are called Muslims.

Jew: a follower of Judaism, the world religion founded in the Middle East about 2000 BC.

libel: to attack a person's reputation, in writing or in pictures.

Nazi: a shortened form of National Socialist, the political party founded by Adolf Hitler. The Nazi party ruled Germany from 1932 until 1945, when Germany was defeated in World War II. Nazi politics are similar to fascism, with a centralized government which allows no opposition. In addition, it is also strongly racist, believing that some peoples are superior to others. They used this belief to justify their anti-Jewish policies.

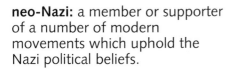

neo-Nazi: a member or supporter of a number of modern movements which uphold the Nazi political beliefs.

Nobel Peace Prize: an award to somebody who has helped bring about international peace. Other Nobel Prizes are given for great achievements in science, medicine and literature.

obscene: immoral, indecent or offensive.

official secret: information that the state will not publish.

philosopher: someone who uses reason and argument to seek the truth and understand the nature of the world and human behaviour.

pornography: words or images which are only intended to arouse sexual desire.

racism: emphasizing the differences between ethnic groups, promoting racial hatred.

sexuality: the way in which a person feels or behaves about sex.

society: human beings, either as a whole or as a group, and how they relate to each other.

Soviet Union: the group of countries and regions united under the control of Communist Russia from 1922. The Soviet Union broke up into independent states in the early 1990s.

terrorist: someone involved in the systematic use of violence and fear to try and achieve a goal.

totalitarian: describes a state that is governed by one central authority which allows no opposition to its rule.

trade union: an organization of workers who work in the same type of employment and who support each other in getting better wages and conditions from their employers.

United Nations (UN): the body of independent countries formed after World War II and designed to act like a world parliament; the founders of the UN hoped to use it to stop further wars and limit human suffering; all the independent nations of the world were expected to join and to try to attain standards of government set by the UN; the UN is funded by contributions from member countries.

whistle-blower: somebody who draws attention to illegal or dangerous actions by their employers.

Useful addresses

In the UK:
Amnesty International, UK Section, 99 Rosebery Avenue
LONDON EC1 4RE
Tel: 0171 814 6200

Christian Aid
35 Lower Marsh,
LONDON SE1 7RG
Tel: 0171 620 4444

Council for Education in World Citizenship
Seymour Mews House
Seymour Mews
LONDON W1H 9PE
Tel: 0171 329 1711

Index on Censorship
33 Islington High Street
LONDON N1 9LH
Tel: 0171 278 2313

United Nations Association
3 Whitehall Court
LONDON SW1A 2EL
Tel: 0171 930 293

And in Australia:
Amnesty International, Australian Section
134 Broadway Road
BROADWAY NSW 2007, SYDNEY
Tel: 02 9281 4188

Australian Red Cross
Red Cross House
159 Clarence Street
SYDNEY NSW 2000
Tel: 02 9229 4111

Equal Opportunity Tribunal
ADC House
99 Elizabeth Street
SYDNEY NSW 2000
Tel: 02 9231 2911

Industrial Relations of NSW
Level 9, Xerox House
815-825a George Street
SYDNEY NSW 2000
Tel: 02 9288 8600

Index